21 SECRETS OF ATTRACTING MONEY

Metaphysical Insights For Physical And Spiritual Wealth—Including 9 Do-It-Yourself Energy Experiments

Erik Tao

21 SECRETS OF ATTRACTING MONEY
Metaphysical Insights For Physical And Spiritual Wealth—Including 9 Do-It-Yourself Energy Experiments
Copyright © 2018 by Erik Tao

Table of Contents

Introduction

"You are the creator; you create with your every thought." This is the key to the law of attraction. Whatever you wish to manifest in your life starts with your thoughts."

–Abraham Hicks

Imagine for a while how wonderful it would be to live a life filled with your deepest desires and dreams—after all, you have all the wealth in the world to enjoy your time to the fullest. Imagine living a fulfilling, stress-free, and gratifying life without any financial constraints. Imagine being the best at what you do and unlocking your true destiny to build wealth, prosperity, and abundance. Perhaps you're now asking yourself, *Can I really live this life?*

Fortunately, the key to unlocking your destiny is in your hands. You hold the steering wheel of your life and can maneuver it in any direction of your choosing. You build your destiny through your thoughts, words, and actions. The wealth creation metaphysical concepts I explain in this book are unfailing, proven, and absolute if done with the correct intention and a powerful belief.

I've had several people come up to me and ask, "Does this really work?" I ask them in turn, "Do you have it in you to make it work?" Nothing works on its own. You have to *make* it work. These are proven principles of wealth creation and abundance successfully used by countless people across the world to build physical as well as spiritual wealth, and there's your proof: it works! However, whether it works for you or not depends on how much you are willing to make it work! Everything works if *you* work. You are completely in control of your destiny and have the potential to attract all you desire in life if you truly believe you are worthy of receiving it.

I don't know where you are currently in life. Maybe it was your last few dollars that you spent buying this book, or you may already be on your way to building riches and fortunes. Irrespective of what you have or don't have currently, you possess the power to control your life and create your destiny. The law of attraction and other powerful metaphysical money attraction secrets have no exceptions. The exception and limitations are in your beliefs and intentions. If your belief is unfailing, these laws will never let you down. When you are in alignment with your deepest desires, it is easy to attract them. Remember, the universe responds to your thought frequencies and energies. Wealth and abundance don't come from outside you. It resides in you in the form of thoughts, energies, and actions.

Before you hold something you desire in your hand, you strongly create energy to attract it within you. You believe and operate with the mindset that it is yours. To bring it into your life, you believe you truly deserve it. This is what the law of attraction and other metaphysical principles are all about. It is about energy transmitted through a strong intention, which helps you attract and manifest your desires.

What can I get from this book? I don't promise overnight riches. No one can. Whoever does is making a big fool out of you. You won't go from ten dollars to a million dollars overnight. However, by applying these wealth creation secrets consistently with the right intention over a period of time, you can engender a transformation in the relationship between you and wealth. You will open your mind and heart to attract abundance, you will align your energies with the universe to receive even more prosperity, and you will increase your chances of living the life of your dreams. Not a bad deal!

We all seek to attract the good things in life, yet we are always playing slaves and victims of destiny. Funnily enough, people will wish for all the wonderful things to happen without even realizing that the power to create what they wish for is within them.

You will understand the principles of metaphysics that elucidate how frequencies created in your mind through thoughts can be utilized to manifest wealth and abundance. If you fixate on a single thing, emotion, desire, or feeling over an extended period, it transforms into your reality. These concepts work equally for everyone if you have the power to believe in them!

Think about it. Why is it that some people have everything in life? They have the best of jobs or businesses, money comes to them effortlessly through multiple channels, they enjoy the best interpersonal relationships—all that while others struggle to go through life, barely making ends meet. If these principles are similar for everyone, why doesn't everyone receive what he or she desires?

Creating wealth and abundance using metaphysical techniques is a powerful process that originates in your mind. The unfortunate aspect of this is that a majority of people are not even aware that they themselves are responsible for the lack of resources in their life. They do not know that they are attracting their own misery owing to their thoughts. We often blame our destiny, other people, or circumstances, among other things, for our misfortunes, little realizing that these have been created by us through both our conscious and subconscious thoughts.

It is a challenge to take the self-limiting beliefs you've held since childhood by their horns and tackle them. If you've been led to believe as children that money is a bad thing, or that it makes people bad, or that you don't need it since there are other more important things in life, you'll have to bring about a huge shift in the way you view money. These self-limiting and incorrect beliefs are so deeply ingrained in us at times that it goes unquestioned and we accept it as truth. When you accept these beliefs as the truth, you don't enjoy a healthy relationship with money, which is why it eludes you throughout your life. I know many who were raised in less than privileged homes and grew up with the belief that "money makes people bad" or "it is the root cause of all evils." These people never really attract wealth and abundance until they consciously align their spiritual energy to attract and wholeheartedly welcome money.

Before you begin reading any further, analyze your beliefs and relationship with wealth. If it's anything other than healthy and positive, you won't be able to make any of these principles work for you. It is your beliefs, energies, intentions, and actions alone that are responsible for attracting or repelling wealth and abundance. In effect, you are pushing away money that is coming your way simply due to the beliefs you hold about it. Isn't this grossly unfortunate?

Stop whatever you are doing right now and make a note about your beliefs regarding money and wealth. Go back to the source. Where did your views and beliefs about wealth originate? Why is money energy negative for you? What are the positive changes you can make in your life, your loved ones' lives, and the world at large with money energy? Do you hold these feelings or emotions about wealth yourself or have they been influenced by another person? Work on transforming your beliefs, feelings, and thoughts about money and you may notice a miraculous transformation in the way it flows to you. Remember, you alone are the author and creator of your destiny!

Secret No. 1: A Seemingly Unimportant Thing

"The feelings of our desires much precede its manifestation."

–Sarah Prout

Do you realize that there are probably thousands of thoughts going on in your mind in a single day? These thoughts have the power to impact your reality and destiny. If you aren't happy with where you are currently in life, you can change your destiny by reshaping your thoughts to manifest your deepest desires. One of the biggest reason people do not attract wealth is that they believe they don't deserve it or that it is something that is beyond their destiny. They believe they aren't as fortunate as the wealthy and successful. In short, their energies are not aligned to attract abundance. It starts with developing a wealthy mindset, and a mindset that has incorrect or self-limiting ideas about money isn't geared for attracting wealth.

We discussed in the Introduction how some people grow up with limiting beliefs about wealth and money. If you believe money makes people bad or that it is the cause of all evil, you share an unhealthy relationship with money. You are therefore, in effect, not aligning yourself to receive wealth from the universe.

The number one secret to manifesting anything in your life, not just money, is to operate with the belief that it is already yours. You don't see it as a far-fetched desire or wish that will be fulfilled in the future. You think, act, feel, and behave like you already have it.

Our thoughts, emotions, and feelings carry a very powerful energy frequency. When you believe something is already yours, you are releasing a strong energy frequency into the universe. Now, on a metaphysical level, the universe is nothing but a mass of energy surrounding us. When you send powerful signals into the universe, it responds with a matching frequency, which means you attract even more of what you strongly believe is already yours.

The feelings or emotions you experience about your deepest desires is the most powerful force in the process of manifestation. These feelings interact with the universe at an energy level. If you feel like something you desire is already yours, your thoughts, feelings, actions, and behavior are in alignment with a positive energy. This positive energy frequency communicates with the outer universe, which then matches your energy frequency by sending you precisely what you desire. Anything your mind conceives, the universe has the power to manifest!

While thinking, feeling, and acting like something is already yours will attract matching energy frequencies from the universe, when you operate with an "I want *something*" belief, you are merely reinforcing the lack of it in your life. You want money because you don't have enough money in your life. This sends a "lack of" energy frequency into the universe, and you end up receiving even more of its lack.

However, in contrast, when you believe that richness, wealth, and abundance are already yours, you send an energy frequency of wealth, abundance, and prosperity and end up attracting even more of it. Do you get the picture? If you think you are poor, you will attract even more poverty. If you believe you have to work really hard to make ends meet, you'll attract even more of this situation. When we perpetually obsess about the lack of something or desperately wanting something (thus reinforcing the lack of it in our life), we continue to lack it.

When do you say you want something? When you don't have something! If you say you want money, you are in effect telling the universe that you don't have enough of it. Start thinking you have everything you want before you truly bring it in your life! This is the biggest secret of the law of attraction.

If you want to attract more wealth and abundance, start by believing it is already yours. Act like you are a millionaire. Dress like one! Talk like one! Observe how millionaires talk, feel, respond to others, and conduct themselves. In your head, you must already be a millionaire because only then will you end up being one.

Secret No. 2: How To See Success

Images have a huge power when it comes to conveying our desires to the universe with intention and purposefulness. They are probably ten times more powerful than words. When you visualize your desires, you don't just send strong energy frequency signals to the universe, you also send them to your subconscious mind, which is a highly potent tool when it comes to manifesting your desires.

When a thought, idea, image, or feeling is strongly imprinted in the human subconscious mind, it guides our actions in alignment with this thought, which helps us create exactly what we desire. How do you send the right signals to the universe and your subconscious mind? Through the power of images and visuals!

Visualization exercises and guided visualization is best practiced early in the morning or just before going to bed. These are the hours when your subconscious mind is most active and can be activated to unlock your true destiny. If you practice visualization exercises just before going to bed, you will give your subconscious mind the right ideas to play around with since it is most active when our conscious mind is asleep.

To practice self-visualization exercises or guided visualization meditation, sit in a distraction-free, quiet, and comfortable place. You can infuse positive energy into the space by lighting candles or burning incense. Assume a relaxed posture. Allow the stress in your body and mind to melt away before you begin. Get into a more positive frame of mind. Close your eyes, and now, start imaging through your mind's eye.

Start by visualizing what you want in explicit detail. Remember, the key is being detailed. The more detailed and precise your visualizations, the greater are your chances of manifesting exactly what you desire.

Let's say for instance you want to increase your company's profits. Be exact when you prescribe visualizations. How much do you want to increase your annual or monthly profits by? Even an increase of $0.50 is an increase. So, if you don't visualize how much you want the profits to increase, you aren't giving the universe or your subconscious mind the exact ideas to work with.

Visualize you profit statement with a profit of a million dollars if that is what you want. How does the profit statement look? How are you holding it in your hand? How do you feel when your company makes a profit of a million? Experiencing these feelings and emotions is integral to the process of manifesting your desires.

Make your visualizations a multi-sensory experience if you want to boost your chances of manifesting what you want. How does your office look after you make a million dollars? How are you and your employees dressed? How does your workplace smell, look, sound, and feel?

There are plenty of guided visualization meditation exercises for attracting more money. The mental images you create through the process of visualization are a projection of your future, which you go through as if it is your present. We learned the importance of believing that something is already ours before we can manifest it. Now, create mental images or visuals of your money goals being fulfilled. Keep in mind, this is the movie of your life. You can't be passive spectators. You play the central role and visualize yourself doing exactly what you want to manifest in life. See yourself enjoying the results of what you desired.

If you want to be wealthy and prosperous enough to travel around the world, see yourself at exotic locations across the planet. Visualize yourself traveling to your dream destinations. If you want money to buy your dream home, imagine your home in explicit detail. How about sitting comfortably by the fireplace and relishing a cup of coffee in your dream home? Or holding the steering wheel of the luxury car you plan to buy? Or sitting in a tropical paradise with a drink in your hand? Give your mind and the universe powerful images to play with so their task in helping you manifest these desires becomes easier. Feel, think, and mentally experience everything you desire.

Visualize the amount of money you wish to make. Do not visualize it as if it's something that you are receiving in the future. See it right now, in your bank account. The exact digits you want. Complete the experience and absorb the feeling of how this figure feels on your bank statement. How exactly do you feel when you have this figure in your bank account?

I know it isn't easy to visualize you are a millionaire when you are currently struggling to pay for your next meal. However, this is exactly what separates the wealthy from the strugglers. The wealthy don't let their current circumstances and challenges spill over into their beliefs about the future. They operate with a powerful belief and intention that it's only a matter of time before they manifest the wealth and life of their destiny. See the magic digit in your account like it exists currently even if you have nothing. This is precisely why some people make the law of attraction work wonderfully for them while others struggle with doing the same.

Experience the exact emotions and feelings that a person does when he has a million dollars on his or her bank account. In fact, go a few steps ahead and start thinking about how you can use the money. What are the things you plan to buy with it? How will you invest it to create even more wealth? Don't most millionaires do this? You are one right now and, like a true-blue millionaire, you should think about how you plan to utilize your financial resources.

I'll share a small story here. A young boy grew up in such poverty that at one point in his life, his family couldn't even afford to live in a proper home. They occupied a trailer parked on the lawns of a relative' house. He toiled for eight hours daily at a factory to fund his education and help support his family.

When things became tough, he dropped out from high school and started taking up odd jobs to feed his family. He began doing stand-up comedy gigs at the local club only to be heckled by the audience.

Fed up of his wretched and miserable life, the lad moved to Hollywood at the age of 21, and the first step he took when he reached Hollywood probably impacted his entire life. The young man drove right up

Hollywood hills in his worn-out Toyota and parked it where he could take sweeping views of the entertainment industry hub along with its dazzling lights. In his head, he visualized himself to be a part of this dream world, entertaining people and making them laugh.

Instead of simply imagining it, the young man did something unthinkable. As a physical reminder of his dream and the exact moment he experienced this desire, he wrote a check to himself for 10 million dollars. His current bank balance was a different story altogether, but that didn't stop him from visualizing his future as if he had already received this amount of money. The check was for "acting services rendered." The young man kept this check as a physical reminder of his dreams in his wallet. Each time he went for a work-related meeting or audition, the check went with him.

The actor went on to receive a princely advance-signing amount for an upcoming film and subsequently went on to make not just his 10 million dollars but much more in the years succeeding. He was confident in his belief that there was no other way but to become a millionaire. He didn't award himself the option of failure. He was dead sure he'd be a millionaire one day. This young man was none other than Jim Carrey. This is a real-life example of the power of visualization and using the power of your intentions to create your destiny.

You have to think something is already yours and visualize it like it is yours before you can transform it into reality.

Secret No. 3: The ONE Emotion To Success

A grateful heart is the most powerful magnet for attracting blessings. There is plenty of power in gratefulness. When you are thankful for something, at a metaphysical level, you are sending a strong positive frequency into the universe. It demonstrates the universe that you have positive frequencies about possessing something in abundance, which helps you attract even more of it. If you want to create more wealth and abundance, be grateful for the money you have, however little it seems at the moment.

If you don't perceive what you presently own with gratitude, there will only be a slim chance of multiplying it. Blessings and complaints both multiply. If you gripe about the lack of something or display an element of ingratitude for what you already have, you are not aligning the energy frequency to receive more of it from the universe. Be thankful for the money and possessions you already own to draw more of them into your realm of reality.

Make a gratitude journal today. At the end of each day, write about 10 things that happened during the day or 10 gifts you feel thankful or blessed to enjoy in your life. Ensure that you add 10 new things to be grateful for each day. It can be anything from the eyes with which you see the beautiful world around you to the feet with which you walk to your workplace. It can be your hands, the roof above your head, the loaf of bread you baked, and your car—just about everything you can and should feel grateful for. Express thankfulness for everything that money can buy you to multiply your wealth and assets.

If your mind is constantly operating with a feeling of being thankful for the wealth you have, your feelings, thoughts, and emotions will be aligned with a powerful energy of thankfulness, thus giving you even more things to be grateful for. Gratitude signifies abundance. By being thankful, you are reinforcing your abundance and attracting even more abundance your way.

Another super wealth attraction tip is to keep a gratitude rock in your pocket, wallet, or purse all the time. Keep it somewhere you can physically and frequently come into contact with it. You can also place it on your work desk or wherever you can spot it prominently throughout the day. Each time you touch the gratitude rock, find something you've bought with your money that you are grateful for. It can be your house, a piece of clothing, a car, a book—anything that you are thankful for receiving from the universe through the means of money. Do this a few times throughout the day, especially before going to bed and on awakening. Think about the wealth and possessions you are truly thankful for.

To create more of what you want, you have to display thankfulness for what you already own. Don't reserve your thankfulness for the future or when you get what you desire. Be thankful for what you have now.

If you have unpaid bills, avoid cribbing about them. It only releases more negativity and attracts even more unpaid bills. Instead, write on the bills prominently, "Thank you universe (or any energy or spiritual force you believe in) for helping me pay this bill." Feel a genuine sense of thankfulness and gratitude for the services you enjoy. Being thankful for the services and feeling happy about paying for them are the keys to clear your bills. If you keep viewing them as a burden or from a point of thanklessness, you'll seldom be able to pay them off. Gratitude is the magic word! Change your relationship with your bills, view these services as a blessing, and you'll seldom be short on money to clear them.

A gratitude rock helps you focus your energies on the present and helps you draw attention to the current moment and blessings. It helps you experience thankfulness for the now and what you have on you presently (clothes, pen, book) to multiply your blessings.

It also helps to switch your thoughts from neutral or negative to positive. If you are in an unpleasant mood, simply being thankful for what you have can instantly lift your spirits or elevate your mood.

You can pick up stone or rock that resonates with you from around a stream, park, or road. I'd strongly recommend selecting a stone that you instantly connect with on a deeper level. You can also buy crystals such as citrine that are known to attract abundance.

Secret No. 4: You Can Do It – Here Is How

Affirmations are positive statements that are said or written multiple times to influence our subconscious mind into believing something as the truth. Words that are spoken in repetition have the potential to firmly embed mental images on the human subconscious mind, thus guiding or influencing our actions in the correct and positive direction. These words motivate, drive, and energize you into creating what you desire.

The mental visuals created by saying these affirmations repeatedly are capable of bringing about a rapid shift in thoughts, ideas, feelings, and actions, thus channelizing our mental energies towards manifesting what we desire. You truly imbibe the feelings and emotions of what you keep saying, which is why these affirmations work wonderfully for manifesting money, wealth, and abundance.

The human subconscious mind is incapable of differentiating between reality and imagination. It believes whatever is imprinted into it as reality. Subsequently, it guides your actions in line with this belief. When you keep saying you are rich, prosperous, and wealthy in a loop, irrespective of what your current financial position is, your subconscious mind accepts it as the truth.

It then guides your actions in line with being wealthy, prosperous, and abundant. You are activating your subconscious mind to operate from a point of scarcity to abundance with a few words or phrases.

Always say your affirmations in the present tense to ascertain that it unlocks the power of your subconscious mind and gets it to guide your actions in the direction of wealth and abundance.

Don't say something as if you are going to accomplish it in the future, such as "I will be rich and prosperous" or "I am going to be wealthy soon." This only reinforces the present lack of it in your life. Your goals aren't placed beyond your reach in the future, they are already yours now!

Stick to positive words and phrases while creating your affirmations. It shouldn't contain any negative words. Our subconscious mind and the universal one cannot at the metaphysical energy level relate to the concept of "not." It simply throws away the no or not and focuses on the energy attached to the words and phrases used.

For example, if you say "I don't want to be poor," the subconscious mind and universal energy will discard the "don't" and focus on the energy attached to poor, thus bringing even more poverty your way.

Instead, say "I am rich, wealthy, and abundant." Use only positive words and phrases about money.

Keep your affirmations personal. Use affirmations that feel good and right to you instead of simply borrowing them from someone else, though you can look on the internet for inspiration. However, you must be able to connect with them on a personal level. Create affirmations that feel right for you.

These positive statements should also be specific, detailed, and unambiguous. Avoid affirming more than one desire in a single statement. You can use different affirmations for different desires. However, clubbing them together in a single sentence can send your subconscious mind and the universe on a wild goose chase. The more detailed and precise your affirmations, the greater are your chances of manifesting it. Reinforce the benefits of manifesting your desires. Precise images help in clarifying your desires to the subconscious mind. Vague affirmations create vague results.

For instance, if you want to increase your business profits this year, you can't simply say "business profits increase." Even an increase in $1 is an increase! How much do you want to increase the profit by? $500? $1000? $100,000? Say "my business profits have increased by (the exact amount)." The ideal time to say your affirmations is when you can see yourself saying it. This multiplies their manifesting energy. Say them while applying make-up, shaving, or getting ready to go to work in the morning. See yourself saying these powerful affirmations while also experiencing the feelings as you do.

Affirmations can also be written several times in an affirmation journal. Allow the feeling to sink while you write. Preferably, use a notebook and a pen instead of a technological application. The process of physically writing something has more impact on the mind because your nerves are directly connected to the subconscious.

Ensure you say your affirmations as many times as possible throughout the day—the more, the better because it will only end up reinforcing the idea more powerfully within your subconscious mind. Say them for a minimum of 20 times, thrice a day. Keep saying it until your subconscious mind accepts it as your true destiny. Make affirmation usage the practice or habit of a lifetime.

Following are a few wealth and abundance affirmations that you can start using right away to attract wealth, money, and abundance.

1. Money, prosperity, and abundance are pouring into my life.
2. I openly embrace and accept wealth, money, and prosperity right now.
3. I am truly grateful to the universe for the overflowing wealth, riches, and abundance in my life.

4. Money flows to me easily and effortlessly.
5. I am a money, wealth, and abundance magnet.
6. Whatever I put my hand on is converted into wealth, riches, and prosperity.
7. I am thankful for limitless riches and wealth that flows my way.

These are just a few examples. Create your own affirmations based exactly on what you want and say them in the present tense by using positive words and phrases.

Secret No. 5:
How To Condition Your Brain For Success (Energy Experiment)

One of the most powerful metaphysical techniques for manifesting your dream destiny is the creation of a vision board. A vision board is a physical or virtual board that represents all our goals, desires, wishes, and visions pictorially. Through images, our vision board depicts what we want in life. We've seen in an earlier chapter how visuals containing powerful energy transmit the right energy frequencies to the universe and our subconscious mind.

By representing your dreams and desires through visuals, you are strengthening and stimulating your innermost emotions because the human mind responds powerfully to visual stimulation. Your feelings and emotions related to the desire then become the vibrational energy that triggers the law of attraction!

Following are some tips to make the most of your vision board.

1. Place your vision board in a place where you can prominently spot it multiple times during the day. It is best if that's the first thing you can see on awakening each morning. Visualization is known to tap into the creative potential of your subconscious mind while programming the brain to spot resources that can lead you closer to the goals you probably didn't notice earlier. Through the metaphysical principles of the law of attraction, your vision board magnetizes or attracts you to situations, people, and opportunities that are needed to manifest your goal. Thus, if your

vision board is filled with visuals of being rich, prosperous, and wealthy, you'll increase your chances of magnetizing people and resources that lead you towards accomplishing your financial goals.

2. Be judicious about the images you pick. Look everywhere from the internet to magazines to brochures and calendars to personal photo albums. Make a beautiful collage out of all the images. Use images that you can connect with on a deeper level. Make the vision board more personalized by adding comic strips, movie dialogues, song lyrics, book quotes, and motivational quotes by famous people that inspire you. I know people who like to use stickers and make sketches to make their vision board even more personalized and power-packed. Do whatever inspires you each time you look at it because you are activating the power of your subconscious mind to send

powerful signals to the universe for manifesting your desires.

3. I would also suggest including positive affirmations about how you feel. Remember your vision board isn't merely about things but the feelings these things evoke in you. Add plenty of positive feelings to the vision board such as abundant, joyful, wealthy, prosperous, financially free, rich, and so on. You should experience these feelings each time you glance towards the vision board. Several successful people I know are in the habit of scanning their vision board just before practicing their visualization exercises and retiring for the day. This helps prompt your subconscious mind to create new insights and ideas while your conscious mind is asleep at night. You'll wake up with a burst of energy and enthusiasm to succeed. Also, you will be guided by your subconscious mind to identify and act on

opportunities that lead you closer to your wealth goals.

4. While there's no limit to what you seek from the universe (and what it bestows you in turn), avoid cluttering your vision board with too many goals and wishes. Keep it limited to 5-6 goals at a time.

5. Get creative with your vision board. I know several people who add several materials, elements, and mediums to their vision board to make it even more power-packed. They use everything from ticket stubs, flowers, brochures, menus, feathers, cloth pieces, and plenty of stuff to represent their true desires.

Secret No. 6: Switch Words (Energy Experiment)

Switchwords are similar to mantras that are chanted to bring about a switch in the energy of your subconscious mind. Though psychotherapist Sigmund Freud first noted the concept of words impacting our subconscious mind, James Mangam created the concept of Switchwords in his book, *The Secret of Perfect Living*. Though the public wasn't ready for this concept at that time, it came back with a bang recently.

Switchwords are nothing but regular, everyday words that are linked to the vibrational frequency that these words generate. They work on the same principles as affirmations. When you keep saying these words in a loop, they talk directly to our subconscious mind. Thus, the power words help in clearing negative blocks that impede our success and activate our capacity to manifest wealth, abundance, creativity, success, and anything else we desire. If there is a negative thought debris that tells you that you don't deserve to be rich and prosperous held within your subconscious mind, Switchwords will help clear it and bring about a more positive transformation in your thought frequencies, thus impacting your actions and opportunities. At times, there are numbers attached to these words, and they come with their own frequency and add to the power of Switchboards.

Switchwords can be used in several ways:

- You can say them repeatedly throughout the day. Say it 20-30 times at least thrice a day to make the most of its powers.
- Switchwords can also be written several times throughout the day.

- They can be used in your artwork or writing.
- Meditate with Switchwords that resonate with you or that you can connect with on a deeper level.
- Some spiritual experts also suggest charging and drinking water (or labeling the water you drink) with these Switchwords.
- They can be written on pieces of paper and kept under your pillow while sleeping.
- Switchwords can also be written on the left side of your body.

The most important thing about using these magic words is they have to be used with the right belief and intention to work. Here are some Switchwords that can help you attract money, wealth, prosperity, riches, and abundance.

- *Find-Count-Divine*: For miracles related to money

- *Shreem*: For attracting wealth and riches
- *Count-Count-Count-520*: For enjoying financial freedom
- *Together-Find-Count-Divine*: For miraculous money-making
- *Add-Count*: To increase or multiply money

Secret No. 7:
Red Wallet

"Abundance isn't something we acquire. It is something we tune into."

–Wayne Dyer

Though it sounds strange at the onset, the color of your wallet or the energy emitted through it can also impact your chances of having money and riches. The Ancient Chinese science of Feng Shui, which talks about the placement and nature of objects in attracting the most positive and powerful energies, lists a few colors that can help your money-manifestation process.

Wallets and purses are known to hold energy because this is where the money you carry is primarily placed. There are plenty of Feng Shui tips to attract money and abundance, starting with the color of your wallet or purse.

According to Feng Shui, since your wallet holds money energy, it should always be treated well. Keep it in great condition, discard all unwanted clutter from it, and keep it in a safe space back home to attract more positive *qi* energy.

Colors possess energy too like everything else, and they stimulate certain psychological responses within our mind. Color psychology is real because it impacts our thoughts, feelings, and emotions at a subconscious level. For instance, notice how the color blue calms you down or green refreshes and rejuvenates your senses. Why not leverage the power of colors when it comes to attracting wealth and abundance?

Red is considered to be the most auspicious color in Feng Shui for attracting money and abundance. It represents the fire element. If you think red is too bright a color for a purse or wallet, try using a combination of reddish black. Red gives you the energy, dynamism, and passion for attracting more wealth-creation opportunities.

The color red also symbolizes strength, power, and success, which means you'll be less likely to spend frivolously. Red can drive or channel your own energy, enthusiasm, and spirit. In Feng Shui, red wallets aren't just known to enhance wealth prospects but also offer good fortune and protection.

Other than red, gold is also considered a classic color for magnetizing wealth, abundance, and riches. The color gold traditionally corresponds with abundance, luck, good fortune, and positivity. The energy, vibrations, and spirit of the carrier that holds your money can considerably impact your wealth-attraction process.

Whether it is energy related to the color red or gold or simply your intention that expects to wholeheartedly receive more money and riches when you use these colors, it is known to work!

Here are some tips to make your wallet luck work for you:

- Keep your purse or wallet clean, neat, and organized all the time. Avoid retaining receipts, expired cards, and other unwanted objects as these impact your wallet energy negatively.
- Store your bills in a well-organized manner to ensure they are placed in the same direction in numerical order.
- Avoid placing your purse or wallet on the floor or ground. Always keep it in a well-organized and positively energized space. Toilets are a big no-no.
- Immediately replace your old and worn-out wallet. You are not holding the right money energy by using a wallet that has undergone wear and

tear. Renew your money luck with a new purse or wallet.

- Ensure that your wallet is never empty. Always have some money in your wallet or purse if you want to attract even more money. At the same time, never overstuff your purse or wallet. Leave some space for more money. Also, ascertain that your wallet is long enough to prevent bills from folding and avoid picking wallets that are strangely shaped. Just ensure it is a regular, long wallet to enable you to keep bills straight.

- Don't let other people borrow your wallet or purse, and never use secondhand purses or wallets. Your money energy should be kept pure and personal.

Secret No. 8: Use UN-logic To Attract Wealth

This isn't just another do-gooder act for earning brownie points. It is a very powerful principle connected to the law of attraction that can help you attract even more when you give.

When you demonstrate generosity and help others, you are only reinforcing your abundance. When do you give or help others with money and other things? When we have excess resources! Some of the world's wealthiest leaders, entrepreneurs, and celebrities helm charitable causes or practice philanthropy because they have plenty of wealth to distribute among the less privileged. This, in turn, helps them attract even more wealth, abundance, and good fortune.

At a metaphysical level, you are communicating an energy of abundance to the universe when you engage in charity or generosity. You operate from a point of abundance and not a point of scarcity, which brings about a huge transformation in your energy. Your acts of kindness and generosity set the stage for you to receive even more from the infinite universal sources.

When we practice acts of generosity, our energy shifts from a state of lack to one of abundance, and a simple shift in energy helps activate our receiving energy.

The simplest and best way to begin is by helping those less fortunate than you. It can be help in the form of money, things, or even service. The help or act of charity can be extended towards a single person or a sector of society. The universe, on a metaphysical energy level, is not concerned about how much you give. Irrespective of how big or little you contribute, you increase your money and good fortune attraction energy.

Don't give with the selfish intention of getting it back from the universe. That is counterproductive to the process of money and wealth manifestation. Set the right intention while giving. When you help someone from a point of genuine compassion, goodness, and love, you create a larger space for receiving abundance, wealth, and happiness. Aim to give selflessly and out of genuine kindness without expecting anything in return, and you'll watch your wealth multiply.

Secret No. 9: Feng Shui

Like we discussed in an earlier chapter, Feng Shui is an Ancient Chinese discipline that dates back more than 3000 years. It was created to balance *qi* (energies) within a specific space. This energy is said to be directly responsible for attracting health, wealth, harmony, and good fortune in our life.

The principles of Feng Shui are rooted in the Taoist view of nature. The principles mentioned in this chapter can be widely used for stimulating the circulation of money, prosperity, and abundance in your life. Here are six simple yet effective ways to align yourself optimally with wealth attraction positions.

1. Keep the kitchen clean. Kitchens are directly linked to your capacity to

attract money in Feng Shui. Everything from the refrigerator to the pantry to the stove should be kept immaculate by storing only the food that is used. Use every burner on the stove. Also, get rid of clutter from the countertops, tables, and islands in the kitchen. A clutter-free, well-organized, and clean kitchen becomes a magnet for wealth.

2. Discard all clutter. This one's huge in Feng Shui because the discipline is based primarily on energies within a space. Space represents opportunities, which means a cluttered space invariably signifies blocked opportunities. By getting rid of unwanted clutter, you'll free the way for money, abundance, and opportunities at the vibration level.

3. Use mirrors and water features. The condition of water in your home directly impacts your finances according to Feng Shui. Never have leaking taps, dripping pipes, or

stagnant water in and around the house as it represents wealth leaving your abode. Broken fountains and other water bodies are not conducive to wealth creation. Avoid water-based art and mirrors that are placed on a height. There should be no hanging mirrors and water-based art above your bed too. It doesn't align with attracting wealth and prosperity.

4. Pay attention to your home office table. Never place it directly against a wall as this represents blocked creative flow, opportunities, and potential. The larger the space opposite your desk, the more opportunities you will attract according to Feng Shui. Arrange your chair so you face an expansive view or keep visitor chairs in front of your desk for attracting money, opportunities, and abundance.

5. Beautify your front door. Wealth and prosperity energies are said to be at your front door. Always keep your

porch area and front door squeaky clean. Avoid keeping broken bulbs or dying plants at the entrance as these signify dead or blocked energy that acts as an obstacle to the flow of money. Increase your money energy by sprucing up the front door, porch, and walkway. Add pretty flowering pots and a dazzling porch light. The area should be well-lit for welcoming greater wealth and prosperity into the household. In Ancient Chinese Feng Shui philosophy, the front door is referred to as the "mouth of *qi*." Its quality and auspicious energy are integral to the Feng Shui of the entire house. You can also use auspicious Feng Shui symbols at the entrance for attracting wealth, good fortune, and abundance.

6. Use the power of your Feng Shui wealth area. According to the traditional school of Feng Shui, your home or office's southeast corner is your wealth or money corner. The

element that rules money and wealth in Feng Shui is wood. Using a flowing water feature like a fountain in your wealth area can activate or facilitate the energy for flowing money and abundance. Placing a jade plant in the area is also a good idea. Use small icons or symbols representing money to increase prosperity. Many people like placing a wealth box in their money or wealth area to activate their money-making power. Use simple materials such as crystals, coins, gems, or anything that signifies money and prosperity. Place all the items in a finely decorated money box, which can in turn be kept in your wealth area.

Secret No. 10: Hollywood

Earlier, we talked about the famous Jim Carrey incident. When Carrey was a young, struggling comedian trying to make ends meet by performing small gigs in Hollywood, he almost gave up on his dreams of becoming a professional actor. After being heckled off the stage following an act at an open microphone session in Los Angeles, he was completely disillusioned and thought he could never be a professional comedian—ever.

Jim sat alone on top of the Mulholland Drive reflecting upon his failures. Suddenly, he did the unthinkable. Jim pulled out a check from his checkbook and wrote himself a check of $10 million. Yes, his current fortune was nowhere close to that figure. The check was written for "acting services rendered."

As I described before, this famous check went everywhere with him. In 1995, after the runaway success of his movies *Dum and Dumber* and *The Mask*, his net worth has gone up to $20 million. That is the power of writing yourself a check. You are carrying positive and powerful energies in your purse or wallet when you write yourself one.

The energies transmitted through this check of abundance have the power to drive your actions and help you seize opportunities at an intuitive, subconscious level. Write yourself a check today of a precise amount and place it in your wallet, purse, or handbag all the time. You'll end up attracting plenty of money-making opportunities!

Secret No. 11:
The Power Of Emotions

My friend who wasn't so wealthy once upon a time had a habit that we all found strange back when we didn't know the powerful principles of the law of attraction and money manifestation. Every once in a while, she'd purchase stuff that would make her feel rich, wealthy, and prosperous. It wasn't just another self-indulgent or preposterous act. It was a way of attracting money on a deeper level. Soon enough, all the things that we thought were beyond her financial reach were easily and effortlessly affordable to her. It was the law of attraction—unfailing and absolute. She attracted all the money, wealth, and abundance in her life because she aligned her energies with being wealthy, which brought even more wealth and good fortune her way.

Every once in a while, save and buy stuff that makes you experience a compelling feeling of being rich and abundant. Splurge on that expensive perfume, designer bag, or bottle of champagne. Next, it could be a lottery ticket or an exquisite jewelry piece—just about anything that makes you feel rich.

Act like you have plenty of money. Imbibe the classy actions and mannerisms of millionaires. Once I learned these powerful money attraction tips, I used to put on my best attire even while heading to the supermarket. People look at you like you are someone rich and prosperous, and this makes you feel rich at an energetic or subconscious level. When you feel rich at a subconscious level through power dressing or accessorizing, you raise your money-attracting vibrations. It is a signal to the universe that you are ready to receive wealth and success—and are dressed up to reach places!

Another super creative tip to feel rich and prosperous is to go to a high-end shopping mall and purchase everything you desire mentally. Experience and absorb the feeling of being able to buy the costliest shoes or the most expensive bag. Get inside the feeling space of the wealthy to transmit the right energy into the universe. How does it feel to purchase everything you want? Mentally buy that $15,000 suit or the mall's most expensive watch. This simple mental act of buying everything you desire will quickly change your money frequencies from scarcity to abundance. Go on and feel like you can buy anything you wish.

Secret No. 12:
1 + 1 = 3 Metaphysical Arithmetic

I've lost count of the number of times I've heard people around me say "I can't afford this" or "It is too expensive for me" or "I don't have enough money to buy it." It isn't a mere coincidence that these people never end up buying the things they say they can't afford.

Stop yourself in the tracks each time you find yourself engaging in self-limiting language patterns. It does more damage to your subconscious mind and vibrations than you can imagine. Replace language patterns of fear, insecurity, and lack of something with more positive and wealthier terms that reframe your subconscious. You can something like "Yes, I will buy this soon" or "I am in the process of buying it" or "This is going to be mine pretty soon." It could also be "I have all the money in the universe to buy it" or other things along that line.

Watch out for the words and phrases you use very closely. Often, they are said so involuntarily that we don't realize their impact on our subconscious. Vocalizing your insecurities, disappointments, and fears only enforces the lack of money and abundance. When you say you can't afford something, you are creating a negative and defeatist vibration about the lack of something in your life. This disillusionment ends up making you feel even more frustrated and disillusioned, which blocks your opportunities and channels of attracting wealth at the subconscious level.

Reframe your powerful feelings and emotions' vibrations by replacing negative and self-limiting terms with winning and positive words and phrases.

I've closely observed the journey of a dynamic entrepreneur who didn't exactly have a very privileged upbringing. When she learned and started to apply the principles of the law of attraction, however, her life began to transform miraculously. Even when her business wasn't going great guns, she posted images of herself with her dream cars at fancy car showrooms only to receive a bunch of congratulatory remarks.

Some people thought it was highly ridiculous on her part to post images as if she'd bought the car when she clearly couldn't afford it. However, she didn't believe she couldn't afford it. In her mind, the universe had already manifested her desires, and it was only a matter of time before she held the steering in her hand. Astoundingly, she went on to buy all those luxury cars over a period of time as her business grew by leaps and bounds. If you want to truly activate the power of the universe in granting you your wish, never believe something is beyond your reach.

The universe will respond to this thought frequency by making the thing even further beyond your reach. Feel wonderful in your heart, mind, and soul by using positive language about money, abundance, and your dream material desires.

Secret No. 13: How to Store Metaphysical Energy

Make yourself energetically aligned and attuned to wealth by using powerful wealth-attraction crystals. Crystals vibrate with the energy of wealth and abundance and are known to have powerful effects on your being. They are known to impact your mind, body, and spirit. Manifesting wealth through the power of crystals opens your heart and mind to recognizing more money-making opportunities with enthusiasm and confidence. You'll experience a greater sense of positivity and possibilities when it comes to magnetizing wealth.

Everything flows when there's passion and positive outlook. Crystals act as energetic supports when you undertake your wealth-creation journey. They are known to work in a unique way to bring more abundance, wealth, and prosperity your way. Combine your powerful intention with these success stones and you will have a wealth attraction technique that can seldom go wrong.

We all know wealth is energy. It often originates from passion, opportunities, beneficial outcomes, and hard work. Below are some of the best wealth, good fortune, and prosperity attracting crystals.

Aventurine

Aventurine is considered one of the luckiest wealth-manifesting crystals. It paves the way for abundance to flow since it symbolizes opportunities and opening doorways to new ventures. The stone will help you move into a more positive money mindset marked by opportunities and possibilities.

Citrine

Few crystals are better than citrine when it comes to curbing negative mental chatter about money. It is known as the ultimate abundance and wealth crystal for its powerful manifestation characteristics. If you want to bring more money, luck, and opportunities your way, citrine helps with its light. It facilitates opening your mindset to embrace opportunities and a positive mindset about money. It is known to be the preferred stone for manifesting since it helps accomplish intentions faster. Citrine is also referred to as the merchant stone for its ability to bring luck and prosperity to entrepreneurs.

Pyrite

Pyrite is perfect for those who tend to feel they aren't worthy of being rich or don't deserve abundance. This dazzling crystal resembles gold with its sparkling, mirror-like appearance. Each time you look at the stone, you'll be inspired to believe on an energetic level that you are worthy of being wealthy and prosperous.

Considered one of the most auspicious crystals for attracting money luck, pyrite is also known to help a person overcome financial hardships and magnetize wealth. It lends you more wisdom, positivity, and confidence when it comes to making important financial decisions. Thus, it guides a person's wealth accumulation in a more positive, subtle, and broader way. You'll find the perspective of your relationship with money transforming drastically.

Note that energized crystals (energized by a professional healer or spiritual master or under the guidance of one) are one of the best ways to attract wealth.

Secret No. 14:
Love your Bills

We've discussed this briefly earlier, but a person who doesn't show their bills the required love and gratitude seldom attracts wealth. Each time a bill lands in your mailbox or email, do not view it as a burden. Like everything else, your bills possess energy. When you express disappointment or annoyance at having to clear another bill, you are increasing your chances of landing in even greater debt because the universe is responding to you with a frequency that matches your own thoughts.

Ensure that you mentally show your bills some love. Express thankfulness to the universe for the wonderful services that you received for those bills. Would you able to speak on the phone or use the internet if your service provider didn't offer you a reliable network? Would you be able to cook or enjoy the benefits of electricity if you weren't offered energy resources by your energy or power service provider? Would you able to fill gas in your car if your credit card didn't help you get by until your salary was credited? Be thankful for all the services you enjoyed in exchange for these bills.

Write "thank you for helping me pay this bill" even if you don't currently have the means to clear it. You are emitting a positive energy signal into the universe about paying the bill, thus increasing your chances of paying the bill soon. If you view it as a troublesome burden, it becomes even more of a burden.

I know people who draw little red hearts on their bills and use these as affirmations of their wealth and prosperity. This allows even more richness, wealth, and abundance to flow their way. Drawing symbols of love and gratitude on the bills and feeling a powerful emotion of thankfulness while doing it will help you pay these bills promptly.

Never send negative energy to your bills. Reframe your perspective of paying bills as an inconvenience to one of gratitude and thankfulness. View these services as a blessing to build up positive energy about them. A simple shift in your perspective can create the most unexpected miracles. Also, keep in mind that over 80% of the world's population survives on under $10 a day and doesn't have access to the services you enjoy. Give that a thought and be grateful for your bills!

Secret No. 15: Rejoice (Energy Experiment)

Yes, finders are indeed keepers, and picking up coins (even little cents) is enough to demonstrate to the universe that you are open to the act of receiving. When you bend down and make an effort to pick money from the ground or floor, you are acting as the custodian of wealth. There is a display of respect and courtesy for money lying on the ground.

Apart from letting the universe know you are open to receiving money, you are also acting as a caretaker for the money you find. I know a lot of people feel self-conscious and embarrassed about picking up coins from the ground or street. Reframe your thoughts. Think about yourself as someone who is giving the money its rightful place.

You are looking after the money. As a conscious, purposeful, and intentional custodian of the cash, you are ensuring that money feels respected and loved. This generates even more appreciation energy, which brings greater wealth and abundance your way.

I also recommend always having a hundred dollar bill in your wallet. The technique finds a mention in Abraham Hicks' book *Ask and It Is Given.* The way it works is that there is always a hundred-dollar note in your wallet or money purse and you are never to spend this hundred-dollar bill. The objective is to experience a feeling of safety and security that there is always money available to you in your wallet whenever you need it. You are mentally spending the money without actually spending it.

The mere knowledge that there is money at your disposal immediately increases a sense of positivity and security where money is concerned. This, in turn, expands your wealth-creation mindset and allows greater prosperity to flow your way.

Each time you find coins on the street or ground, bend down to pick it up and rejoice. Celebrate the act of finding money and being its custodian. You will end up attracting more money!

Secret No. 16: Light A Candle (Energy Experiment)

Lighting candles is a great way to grow your physical and spiritual wealth. You'll not only increase your chances of magnetizing wealth and good fortune, you'll also experience a spiritual high. It elevates your mood, positive spirit, and clear thinking. Besides, the fragrance of candles lends an intensely positive aura to your space. Infuse your space with a spiritual aura by lighting some.

I highly recommend creating an abundance altar. It can be any sacred space that you feel good about or experience a connection with. In effect, you are using it to worship money or the money gods and goddess. Light a candle every morning and evening while praying, meditating, or doing your visualizations. Remember, your soul responds on a deeper level to these energies to activate your money-making potential even further.

Set the atmosphere for your soul and subconscious mind to respond. Pick a candle that has a wonderful, positively energizing fragrance that you can connect with success and prosperity on a deeper level.

An energized green candle is considered best for attracting money, wealth, and prosperity. Green is also the preferred color for conducting money and prosperity spells. Since green symbolizes new beginnings, it can revive your not-so-pleasant financial fortunes and transform it into more positive beginnings.

Here is an example of a money and abundance spell performed using a green candle. Pick a new green candle and generously anoint it with lavender, cinnamon, or any other oil. Lavender is the most popular oil for performing money spells. Ensure you like or feel positive about the fragrance of the oil you use because these spells are all about transferring energy. You will in effect transfer a part of your personal energy into the candle, and it won't be effective if you don't like the oil.

Take a paper and mention your desire for more money, prosperity, and good fortune on it. Be fully focused on your heart's deepest desires. Now, light the candle and simply visualize that your desires and wishes are being manifested. Imagine how it'll be to have what you want. Focus on the flame of the green candle to hold your thoughts. Ensure your mind is free from distractions, disturbing thoughts, and self-limiting belief or ideas. You should completely believe in your ability to manifest wealth and abundance with the right intention for the technique to work.

Once you are done visualizing your desires, fold the paper and put it into the candle flames. Watch it light up. Allow it to be collected on an ashtray or vessel. Don't put off the fire; just allow it to continue burning naturally. Most money spells are conducted on Thursdays as they are believed to be the most auspicious days for attracting abundance, wealth, and prosperity.

Another popular spell involves the use of a couple of candles. One is a green candle while the other is metallic gold. The spell has to be done during the waning moon period on a Thursday. To begin, energize both candles. Apply money oil generously on it as you visualize a part of your own energy being transmitted to these candles. Later, carve the words "money" and "prosperity" on the candles. Now, shut your eyes and focus on the visualization. Visualize yourself being wealthy, rich, and fortunate. Pray to the candles to help you magnetize wealth. Finally, snuff the candles.

Secret No. 17: The Make-A-Bigger-Cake Principle

One of the biggest obstacles to the process of any spiritual attraction is eliminating negative, self-limiting thoughts. A mentally, spiritually, and psychologically healthy individual can place their intention into anything they desire and accomplish the outcome quickly and in a hassle-free manner.

If you consistently place your intention into the abundance, wealth, and lifestyle you desire, you will increase your chances of attracting it.

Are your thoughts in alignment with what you expect? What are the exact thoughts, beliefs, and emotions you expect while focusing on your desires?

Doubts, uncertainty, negative expectations, hopelessness, and low self-esteem end up blocking the flow of your spiritual energy. It is important to clear personal challenges if you truly want to attract more wealth and abundance in your life.

What does a mechanic do when you take your car to him or her? They won't immediately look for ways to boost the performance of your vehicle. Their top priority will be to find out what's wrong with the vehicle and take measures to rectify it.

Take the same approach when it comes to attracting more wealth in your life. Do you have any negative or self-limiting beliefs about money that are blocking your path to wealth and abundance? Identify these self-limiting beliefs and work to eliminate them. If you share an unhealthy relationship with money or view it in a negative light, work to change your perspective about money. If you see it as the root cause of all evil or think all wealthy people are bad, change your view.

Also, feelings of jealousy about other people's wealth and good fortune will seldom help you attract more money. Be genuinely happy for others. Believe that you will also be a recipient of their good fortune. Be happy for and cheer on other people's success. Feel joy in their joy. This way, you are transmitting positive energies about other people's success and money, which will in turn impact your own success, abundance, and good fortune.

Secret No. 18:
How To Write Your
Success-Script

If you want to increase your chances of manifesting your dreams, be crystal clear about what you want. The universal or spiritual forces, or anything else you like to call them, are *not* known for dealing with mixed or ambiguous messages. When you don't have a clear vision of what you seek, you reduce your chances of manifesting it. If you want stellar results, be precise about what you desire. The universe responds brilliantly to exact wishes and desires! Similarly, avoid changing your mind about what you seek from time to time. It sends the universe on a wild goose chase and doesn't help you manifest your heart's desires.

Think of it like this. What do you do when you order from a catalog? What if you just say you want something blue and big? Or if you end up returning an illegibly filled order form? How about an order form written with multiple confusing requests? You will either end up receiving something you didn't want or nothing at all.

The universe has a catalog of wishes. If you don't point to the exact image and simply offer vague descriptions about what you want, it will get confused. Again, if you keep sending it conflicting, confusing, and vague images about what you want, you are less likely to manifest your desires. Clarify your money, wealth, and abundance goals before you expect to receive from the universe.

What exactly do you seek to accomplish in the next month, six months, or year where monetary or wealth goals are concerned? What car (exact brand, model number, color, etc.) do you wish to own in the coming year? How does your dream house look? What is its entrance, interiors, windows, doors, furnishings, furniture, decorations, kitchen, bathroom, bedrooms, curtains, paintings, beds, floors, walls, and gadgets like? Yes, you've got to be that specific.

You'll be blown by accounts of people who visualize their dream house in graphic details (including the colors of its walls and the hardware) and get exactly what they visualized. Start being as detailed and precise about your dreams and visions as you can!

Secret No. 19: Intention Box (Energy Experiment)

Our words and phrases have magic—that is why it's called *spell*ing, isn't it? Writing about your intentions while focusing all your positive energy is a great way to manifest them. You already have a vision board in place. The next energy experiment to compliment it is to create a wealth intention box.

Begin with a beautiful and meaningful box. You can buy one, but I always recommend creating one to establish a more personal connection with it. This is also a wonderful project to undertake as a family. Next, mention your intentions on individual pieces of post-its. The intention can be any wealth, money, and prosperity-related goal. You may want to increase your company profits or desire a pay hike or earn more passive income.

Ensure that you utilize only positive words and terms while avoiding negative words and terms such as "no" or "not." "I don't want to be in debt" can be reframed as "I want to be financially free." After each intention, write something like "Grant me this or something even better Universe."

With this statement, you are stating that you are open to receiving limitless unexpected opportunities and possibilities. This box can be updated every few weeks or months on new moon days, which are known to have powerful creativity and wish-fulfilling energy. This is a fun and enjoyable way to put the law of attraction into practice and see what you end up manifesting.

Secret No. 20:
Gratitude Jar
(Energy Experiment)

We saw in an earlier chapter how gratitude has increased vibrational energy. A gratitude-filled heart thus becomes a magnet for miracles. When we are grateful for what we currently have, we multiply our blessings. Our energy vibrations instantly rise and become a creation match at all levels. A gratitude jar is a more spiritual experiment that consciously expresses gratitude for each day. This is another individual or family money-manifestation experience designed to multiply your blessings.

Begin with a big jar and prominently put a "gratitude" label on it. You can decorate or beautify the jar as you desire for a more personalized connection. Every day on a tiny piece of paper, mention something your money could buy or something you already have that you are truly grateful for.

When the gratitude jar is full, review everything you are thankful for during the week or month. This one practice is capable of changing your entire life. It aligns you with a positive energy and completely changes your perspective from lack of to limitless and genuine appreciation. It is one of the best ways to activate your money and wealth energy not only to draw new blessings but also to multiply what you currently have.

Secret No. 21:
Mr. Money
(Energy Experiment)

This is another simple yet effective money-manifestation experiment. Begin by imagining Money as a person—a real individual with feelings, emotions, and energies. Create a vision of Money's persona if you like. What does Money look like? Is it a man with grey eyes and a red cloak? Or is it a woman with blue eyes and a black coat? Be as detailed as possible.

Now, write a letter to Mr. or Ms. Money. Tell Money all that you thought about him or her. Pour your heart out about your relationship with each other, perhaps about how he or she had kept you away from a toy you desperately wanted as a child, how you disliked him or her for not being able to buy the dress for your school function, or how you always wanted Money yet he or she was never around. Write about your relationship with money going back to your childhood.

Often, our negative view of money or the unhealthy relation we share with it is directly responsible for our inability to attract wealth and abundance. When you freely express your feelings about money, you release all the pent-up negativity to establish a fresher and more positive bond. This change in your relationship or equation with money helps you pass on the right energies to receive wealth and abundance.

Once you've expressed your true feelings about money, it is easier to realign your feelings and energies about money, which will make you more receptive to it. You'll start sharing a healthier relationship with it, and this will help you attract even more.

After expressing your inherent and deeply held negative beliefs about money, start writing love letters to money. Tell Mr. or Ms. Money how much you adore and appreciate its presence in your life. Tell Money how thankful you are for the wonderful things it helps you buy or the ways through which it changes your life. Address Money as your confidante—as an ally who helps you accomplish your goals.

Keep doing this money experiment over a period of time and you'll begin noticing the changes in the way wealth responds to you.

Bonus Secret: Manifestation Technique (Energy Experiment)

Some folks, despite studying everything about manifestation, struggle to create the material and spiritual wealth they want because they lack intention or a consistent routine. Here is a 7-day manifestation technique that helps with intention setting, being consistent, and silencing all the noise around you.

People often complain that they are overwhelmed by the noise outside them—that they don't get time to complete tasks or even focus on what they want! At times, we are so busy working that there isn't much time to manifest our innermost dreams and desires. Sounds familiar?

The reality is that we are often focusing so much on our outer world or our immediate environment (which consumes a majority of our attention, intention, and energy) that we are left wondering why we don't get what we truly desire.

Let's say you print an article on a piece of paper. You find some mistakes and whiten it. Then, you reprint it. However, the mistake still stays. How? Well, you'll have to make changes to the digital copy, not the outer paper copy. We can't modify our outer world until we bring about changes in our inner world. Everything originates from within. Everything you've manifested or plan to manifest originates from inside you.

Start afresh from within: do this 7-day wealth-manifestation experiment.

1. Pick any three money or wealth related goals that you want to manifest over the next 7 days. It could be a new project or getting

money from a deal or simply earning more wage during the week.

2. Next, visualize each desire or goal as if it has already been fulfilled or granted to you.

3. Lastly, mention your results when thanking the universe and acknowledging yourself as a strong creator of your destiny. If you want greater accountability for following these steps or sharing it with the world, I'd recommend writing a blog to track your manifestation success.

Bonus Secret: Intention Technique (Energy Experiment)

This simple yet highly effective experiment demonstrates how you impact the world and how you can magnetize your goals and desires based on thoughts, beliefs, feelings, and expectations. The world surrounding you reflects on your beliefs, feelings, and expectations. You come across what you really want to see.

This experiment will demonstrate how your intentions rule what you see and how you experience around the world. It proves that you will find what you genuinely seek or look for and, ultimately, that you can manifest or find anything you seek. It will help you realize that no matter how unrealistic or impractical your current wealth goals appear to be, with the right intention, you can manifest just about anything.

1. In the next 72 hours, actively look for a single specific item. You can use anything from purple cars to bluebirds to bird feathers to a brown horse to pink boxes—just pick something specific.
2. Make an intention of spotting your red boxes or brown horses in the next 72 hours. "I genuinely and truly intend to see brown horses in the next 72 hours."
3. Now, closely watch out for all the brown horses you come across in the next 72 hours. Make a note each time you spot one. You don't have to see physical brown horses. They can be visuals in a magazine or pictures on your social media feed. It could be a pattern on a shirt. Actively watch out for the brown horse imagery. Record your results in a journal or a blog.

4. You'll find yourself coming across more brown horses than usual because you are operating with powerful intention energy. This will work the same way for the process of money-making and wealth creation.

Conclusion

I sincerely hope you enjoyed this book and were able to take away several proven strategies for increasing your chances of manifesting wealth, prosperity, and abundance and lead the life of your dreams. Remember, you are in charge of your money and prosperity destiny, and the key to unlocking or activating your money-making powers is within you alone.

I've included lots of real-life examples, practical wisdom, actionable tips, and to-do nuggets to help boost your chances of unlocking or activating powerful principles of wealth manifestation right away. However, you won't accomplish the life of your dreams simply by reading about the power metaphysical principles described in the book. Knowledge without application is futile!

Start implementing the techniques and methods mentioned in the book to unravel your true glorious destiny. Bring about a shift in your mindset and the way you view money to experience a complete transformation in your fortunes. Similarly, take action towards fulfilling your financial goals on a daily basis.

You can't just manifest money by sitting and visualizing money falling into your lap. The law of attraction has to be backed by concrete action if you truly want to manifest your goals.

Finally, if you enjoyed reading the book, please take some time to share your views and post a review. It'd be highly appreciated.

Here's to accomplishing all your goals and leading a wealthy, financially rewarding, and meaningful spiritual life of your dreams!

www.ingramcontent.com/pod-product-compliance
Lightning Source LLC
LaVergne TN
LVHW020345200726
843507LV00012B/2508